Dedicated to the young corporate professional

Copyright © 2012 Ram Iyer

All rights reserved. No part of this book may be used or reproduced in any manner whatsoever without written permission of the author and publisher.

Printed in the United States of America

ISBN-13: 978-1475009286

ISBN-10: 1475009283

First Edition

The Career Journey Pocketbook

Table of Contents

Prioritize career success 11
No "work-life balance" 12
Operate in your C-Zone 13
Compasses…not maps 14
Not money…not titles 15
Degrees are just tickets 16
The ROT league conundrum 17
Forget entitlements 18
Memorize 30-30-30-10 19
You were hired because… 20
Gain your boss's trust 21
Remember Darwin 23
Blue-chip beware 24
Hop jobs…frequently 25
Read Google's take on job hopping 26
Don't become a boiled frog 28
MBA as a door-opener 30
Get your MBA in your 20s 31
After your MBA, hop! 32
Solve problems or deliver with impact 33
Differentiate yourself 34
Chase "wow" projects 35
Join winning teams 37

Rotate jobs	39
Learn from failures	40
Mimic a Canadian goose	41
Unleash the Change Agent	42
The magic of *WIIFM*	43
Wear 'em down	44
Communicate often	45
The 30% Support Rule	46
Use mini-goals	47
Personalization magic	48
Use PowerPoint wisely	49
The matchbox rule	50
Be an effective storyteller	51
Adopt loss aversion	52
Right-size your team	53
Know your customer	54
The power of stopping	55
Focus on the "*what* else?"	56
Emotional neutrality	57
Perception—the silent killer	58
Show active support	59
Energy + Extroversion	61
Align with your boss	62
Decision-making logic	63
Appreciating Sprezzatura	64
Take a contrarian position	65

Facts are useless 67
Speak up! 68
Be unpredictable 69
Know when to shut up 71
No alibis 73
Be comfy looking dumb 75
Choose the right boss 77
Be "ha-ha" funny 78
Think like a CEO 79
Be a process expert 81
The back-pocket panacea 83
Index 84
Acknowledgments 86
About the Author 87

Why read this book?

We are living in a world of speed. We want tomorrow's "yet-to-be-defined" needs to be fulfilled today, instantly. If you are holding this book in your hands, you are probably one of the many corporate professionals who are seeking a quick elixir that can tell you what to do RIGHT NOW to rise up the career ladder.

The rationale behind reading this pocketbook is no different than the rationale behind reading the full version of my earlier successful book, *The Career Journey*, with the only exception that this pocketbook will get straight to the career tips sans all the jazz. Follow these distilled tips based on my twenty years of corporate America experience and start reaping the fruits right away.

Tip 1

Prioritize career success

To achieve career success, you have to live and breathe the idea of achieving corporate career success day in day out. It has to be the only vision and mission of your life. If you have any other competing priorities, your chances of achieving career success are extremely limited.

Tip 2

No "work-life balance"

Career-oriented professionals realize that the phrase "work-life balance" is utopian and does not exist. They simply replace the phrase with a more realistic one, "*work-life tradeoffs.*" Achieving career success means you have to trade-off personal life for corporate life.

Tip 3

Operate in your C-Zone

The *C-Zone* is the "Career Success Zone" where your talents, passions, and organizations (the companies you admire) overlap. Determine your C-Zone and take a job that has the highest overlap with your C-Zone. This is the zone where your chances of career success are the highest.

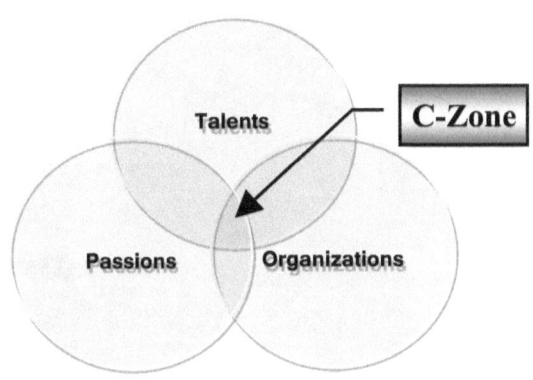

Tip 4

Compasses...not maps

Manage your career plan like a compass, not a map. Every career role is an opportunity that leads to more opportunities. Select roles that are aligned in the general direction leading to your personal C-Zone, where you would be operating at your highest level of effectiveness and passion.

Tip 5

Not money…not titles

Neither money nor job titles should ever be the driving force behind career decisions. Money or title should just be coincidental. Your talent and passion for the job should be the most important things. Once you have these two key requirements for success, the rest comes automatically.

Tip 6

Degrees are just tickets

Your education and degrees are table stakes. They are just tickets to participate in the race to win the job. Once you are in the job, the value of your degree goes out the door. From then on, what truly matters is *everything else*. The higher-up the ladder you go, the less important your education becomes.

Tip 7

The ROT league conundrum

Any university that is not among the very top in the nation belongs to the ROT league. ROT stands for "Rest of them." Do not waste too much time deciding between schools in the ROT league. It will not matter in the long run, because as seen from the eyes of the employer, all schools in the ROT league are the same.

Tip 8

Forget entitlements

No one is automatically *entitled* to anything in the corporate world. The sooner you drop this word from your dictionary, the sooner you will be at peace with yourself. Remember that promotions are usually the result of collective decisions. Unilateral decisions are rare in most well-run organizations.

Tip 9

Memorize 30-30-30-10

Your career growth rate is influenced by four variables with different levels of contribution. Your ability to do the next job level makes up 30%; your ability to get along well with people is another 30%; your ability to help the boss achieve his goals is another 30%; and lastly, your educational background makes up a mere 10%!

Tip 10

You were hired because…

Always know the answer to the questions:

- *Why did the organization hire me?*
- *Why did the current boss hire me?*

Remember that the organization did not hire you because you have a MBA. They hired you because they believe you can show results.

Tip 11

Gain your boss's trust

All things considered, the most important person in your corporate life and influencer of your career success is your immediate boss. If you try to outsmart and run over and above your boss, you will be destined for failure more frequently than not.

Never underestimate the influence and power that your boss can have in shaping your career path, no matter how little influence your boss may seem to have. The mere position of your boss in the organizational hierarchy provides him or her with access to information before you—information that can be used against you, if needed. However, if you align your goals with that of your boss, and constantly prove to him or her that you can be the most trusted advisor or ally, the odds of your success are significantly improved.

Tip 12

Remember Darwin

Your flexibility, readiness and responsiveness to change are the ultimate tests of your career success. Remember one of the most famous quotes of Charles Darwin:

> *"It is not the strongest of the species that survive, nor the most intelligent, but the ones most responsive to change."*

Tip 13

Blue-chip beware

Blue-chip organizations can be the best places for learning best practices, and they also provide excellent opportunities to learn many different functions throughout the organization via job rotations. However, when it comes to speed when rising up the ladder, they are not the best bet. Blue-chips get you closer to a work-life balance lifestyle.

Tip 14

Hop jobs…frequently

You have an optimal *Hop Zone*, which is defined as your own personal age range when you have the highest level of independence to pursue your wants. Make use of your Hop Zone and change jobs frequently. You should experience at least 5 different good roles, preferably in different companies, before you are 35 years old!

Tip 15

Read Google's take on job hopping

Judy Gilbert, a director of "people operations" at Google™ said in an interview with Fast Company™:

> *"We're going to look very differently at a resume where somebody hops from company to company but in a similar job. That's not such a great story versus someone who's getting promoted or building their scope. We want evidence of somebody who is growing. I want to hear the plan they had in mind: I liked what I was doing, but I didn't*

have the depth in design that I needed, so I consciously took this next job with a small design firm."

Remember that the quality of your experiences in terms of breadth and depth is key to job hopping, not merely the act of hopping for the sake of hopping!

Tip 16

Don't become a boiled frog

One well-known and documented observation is that of a frog and its reaction to boiling hot water. A frog thrown into a pan of room temperature water can be boiled to death if the temperature is slowly increased. The same frog would jump out really fast if the frog was thrown directly into a pan of boiling water.

You do not want to be like the frog in room temperature water slowly being boiled to death. Be constantly vigilant and prepared to hop jobs, even in the face of moderate changes in the environment. Do not just hop when you are thrown into boiling water. It may be too late and you may not survive because if the heat does not get you, the fall surely will.

Tip 17

MBA as a door-opener

A MBA can be a good degree to change your career path if the current path is not aligned to your *C-Zone*, the zone where you operate at your highest level of performance. A MBA degree can open new doors into new areas that may otherwise be closed. However, the full usefulness of a MBA depends on what you do after you get your MBA!

Tip 18

Get your MBA in your 20s

The usefulness of your MBA degree significantly depends on your age. The optimal age to get your MBA is between 25 to 30 years, with a higher preference for 25 over 30. Getting your degree earlier provides you with more time to hop companies and roles faster with a higher success rate before Anti-Hopping Forces come into play.

Tip 19

After your MBA, hop!

If career growth and more money are part of the reason you obtain a MBA, it is best to hop as soon as you graduate with your MBA. Staying in the same company rarely yields any incremental benefit post your MBA degree.

Tip 20

Solve problems or deliver with impact

Merely stating facts has zero value in today's world because information is easily accessible anywhere, anytime. That leaves you with only two options:

- *Solve big complex problems*

    or

- *Deliver factual messages with emotional impact.*

Tip 21

Differentiate yourself

Differentiate yourself from your competition to rise up the career ladder. The quality and quantity of your experiences are allow you, as an individual, to distinguish yourself daily, so take on work and projects TODAY that will differentiate you when the right opportunity knocks at your door TOMORROW.

Tip 22

Chase "wow" projects

A "wow" project has the following attributes:

1. It matters.
2. It makes a difference.
3. It transforms the organization.
4. It showcases your strengths and the value you bring to the organization.
5. It is "real" and not hype.
6. It impacts many stakeholders.
7. It is rare.
8. It has upper management visibility.

If you ever come across the opportunity to lead such a project, don't hesitate for even a moment. Leading such a project will help you learn new skills, become business savvy, build networks with the people that matter, and most importantly, set you up for future promotional opportunities. Yes, it will come with its baggage of higher stress levels and late nights, but it will serve you well in the long run.

Tip 23

Join winning teams

Find a winning team in your organization and join the team. A winning team has the following attributes:

1. A laser-like focus on results.
2. A solid track record of implementing "wow" projects.
3. Comprised of good talented employees.
4. A solid leader who invests in the team's strengths and plays an active role in the employees' career trajectories.

5. Diversity in composition contributing to complementary strengths.

A lot of your career success depends on the company you keep. Winning teams with talented employees who implement "wow" projects is where all the real action and learning happens. Find one and get your way in!

Tip 24

Rotate jobs

Job rotations are excellent ways to gain new knowledge from new experiences. They also provide opportunities to apply your proven skills in a new role, and thereby differentiate yourself. Remember that experience is not about the number of years on a job; it is ultimately about the number of different experiences and wins you have in your career.

Tip 25

Learn from failures

Failure is a critical requirement for success. Failures teach us what not to do—an important element of a good experience. Once you have a strong knowledge of what not to do, the decisions you make, or actions you take, have a much higher probability of success.

Remember the quote of physicist Niels Bohr:

> *"An expert is a man who has made all the mistakes which can be made, in a narrow field."*

Tip 26

Mimic a Canadian goose

Canadian geese are known for their seasonal migrations in a V-shaped flight formation. They are successful in these long migrations because birds take turns in leading the team. Every bird has to be leader at some point. If not, the migration fails.

Like Canadian geese, you have to learn to lead and go to the front as often as you can. If you do not learn to move to the front, you will always remain a follower. Don't play it too safe.

Tip 27

Unleash the Change Agent

Change Agents thrive on conceiving and implementing changes in business processes that help improve the bottom-line of organizations. They are creative, and work with a purpose in mind. They do not work in a vacuum. They get things done through people. If you want to succeed in your career, unleash the change agent in you!

Tip 28

The magic of *WIIFM*

Changing any person to your way of thinking is all about knowing the fact that every person comes to the table with just one question in his or her mind, "What's in it for me?," better known by its acronym *WIIFM*. Remember this and you have conquered one of the most fundamental rules of influencing people, no matter what the situation. It is never about you. It is always about them.

Tip 29

Wear 'em down

"Have a bulldog persistence on issues that matter to you," says author Tom Peters. If you are persistent, emotionally committed, and willing to battle on and on, it will wear your enemies down. They will either choose a different turf for their battles, or they will take your side when on your turf. Persistence, energy, and passion are rare and contagious. Take them with you wherever you go.

Tip 30

Communicate often

Communication is key to success in all positions of leadership and management. The people you wish to change will refuse to change unless you reinforce, on multiple occasions, that change is needed, and is good for them and the organization. You will never be blamed for over-communication. It is the best hedge against failure.

Tip 31

The 30% Support Rule

When you try to change others, quite often they look for outside help to guide the decision. If you want to sell an idea to 10 people, try to sell it to the 3 most popular ones separately, in individual, one-on-one sessions. Use their support to convince the remaining 7 people to your way of thinking. The odds of selling the concept increase dramatically with this simple strategy.

Tip 32

Use mini-goals

Break down large and complex goals into smaller goals called mini-goals. These are much more easily, and quickly achievable. Successfully achieving your mini-goals generates momentum and optimism in the team. The small wins help propel the team forward until the larger goal becomes a reality.

Tip 33

Personalization magic

Today's consumers crave personalized experiences. Your team members should feel an emotional connection to the project. They should be convinced that their time, investment, and support for your project is catering to their personal needs. If not, they will not invest their costly time.

One way to help is to give your project a name that makes it appealing.

Tip 34

Use PowerPoint wisely

PowerPoint can be used as a great tool to sell your story to the intended audience. Learn the tricks of how to be effective at creating and delivering PowerPoint presentations. Read a few good books on PowerPoint and craft a personalized list of PowerPoint rules for creating effective presentations. This will serve you well in life.

Tip 35

The matchbox rule

When it comes to writing or delivering speeches, it is prudent to remember what Dwight Eisenhower told his speechwriters:

> *"If you can't put the bottom-line message on the inside of a matchbox, you're not doing your job."*

Do you know what your simple one-liner version of your bottom-line message is? If not, think it over again.

Tip 36

Be an effective storyteller

Marketing genius, Seth Godin, coined the word "*ideavirus*" for ideas that spread. To create your own ideavirus, be a fantastic storyteller. People love stories. Ideas conveyed using stories as the backdrop always spread faster, which is precisely what you want to happen for success.

Tip 37

Adopt loss aversion

Remember that people generally are more interested in avoiding losses than acquiring gains. Instead of saying "If we implement this idea, we will save $1 million," rephrase it as "If we do not implement this idea, we will lose $1 million." One simple twist to the same message and you get a line of supporters!

Tip 38

Right-size your team

Team size is crucial to team success. A team is too small if it lacks *key* members that allow it to be effective and make optimal decisions. On the other hand, a team is too large if it has too many *extra* members that lead to too many opinions and delayed decisions. Remember that "*A camel is a horse designed by a committee.*"

Tip 39

Know your customer

No matter what you sell, you have to remember your customer. What are their needs? A BMW or Benz salesperson sells a *lifestyle*, not an automobile. The same salesman has to change the message if he is selling a Kia or Toyota instead to a different customer. What is your customer looking for? Understand that first, very intimately, before you attempt to sell your product.

Tip 40

The power of stopping

Change does not always mean the need to start something new. Equally important is what you have stopped doing over the last year. Are there non-value added processes that you see being done just because someone said so many years ago? Find them and stop them! That means a lot to the company's bottom-line, and thereby, your reputation as a change agent!

Tip 41

Focus on the "*what else?*"

You are in a ruthlessly competitive word. Your competitors are global. All of a sudden, you find yourself in a vulnerable position with not enough selling points. This is precisely why you need to start asking "*What else?*" questions:

- *What else is a differentiator?*
- *What else can I deliver that my competition cannot?*
- *What else …?*

Tip 42

Emotional neutrality

One of the key attributes of successful people is that they rarely make decisions impulsively. The greater the impact of the decision, the more thought is put into the decision making process. In other words, make key decisions while in an emotionally neutral state.

Tip 43

Perception—the silent killer

If you hear a certain piece of feedback consistently and you don't agree with it, it does not matter what you think. The truth is, you are being perceived that way. If you are perceived the same way by the key decision makers who control your career progression, your chances of rising up the ladder are limited. It is high time you fix that perception.

Tip 44

Show active support

A common tactic adopted by many is to remain silent when you truly agree with a speaker's viewpoint. The speaker may be your peer, your boss, or anyone for that matter. If you consistently speak only when you disagree, then you render a perception that you are always confrontational and oppositional to new viewpoints. This is because the various speakers never see you actively support or say "yes" to anything. The only image they have of you are when you say "no," or are disagreeable.

Actively supporting a position that you truly like is a simple way to neutralize that negative perception. If you support something, show it, and increase your positive image at the same time.

Tip 45

Energy + Extroversion

In his book, *Winning*, Jack Welch writes:

> "*Differentiation favors people who are energetic and extroverted and undervalues people who are shy and introverted, even if they are talented. I don't know if it is good or bad but <u>the world generally favors people who are energetic and extroverted</u>.*"

It is a rarity to find a leader who is introverted or lacking energy. Can you think of even one leader with either of those traits?

Tip 46

Align with your boss

The more you are aligned with your boss, the more trust your boss has in you, and the more you get rewarded in time. If you have an opinion that is contrary to your boss, offer it in a tactful manner. One strategy is to make it seem like you are offering, but not actually making the decision on behalf of your boss. The moral: *Agree with your boss almost all the time.*

Tip 47

Decision-making logic

Remember that the decision making logic at the higher levels of management is different than at the lower levels. At the lower levels of an organization, the decisions and activities are *script driven*. At the higher levels, decisions are a result of *opinion coalitions,* hence not that simple and straightforward.

Tip 48

Appreciating Sprezzatura

Sprezzatura is a beautiful Italian word that means:

> *"A certain nonchalance, so as to conceal all art and make whatever one does or says appear to be without effort and almost without any thought about it."*

Sprezzatura is the ability to accomplish difficult actions with flair, and to hide the conscious effort that goes into them.

Roger Federer displays *Sprezzatura*! Do you? If not, embrace it sooner than later.

Tip 49

Take a contrarian position

Do not repeat what other people have already stated. There is nothing original in repeating or just agreeing with someone. However, if you do not agree with the position of someone in the team, do not hold yourself back from taking on a contrarian position.

Most good leaders like to see younger, entry-level employees stand on their feet and offer their opinion on something, or argue against convention, or the wisdom of the day. They like to see someone defend a position with passion and energy. Good leaders like to see you be yourself. So, if you want to be seen positively by the top leaders of your organization, take a contrarian position and defend it with passion and energy.

Tip 50

Facts are useless

Facts are useless. Facts and information are easy to find in our world of Google™ searches and Wikipedia™. This means that simply imparting facts and figures will not put you in a position of power. Anyone can do that. You have to differentiate yourself by being original. Say something that no one knows or is not public knowledge.

Tip 51

Speak up!

Opportunities come in many forms. However, the really good opportunities are those where a critical business problem is being discussed and solutions sought. If you wish to be seen as a leader in your company, you have to learn to speak up when such a good opportunity presents itself. The bigger the stakes, the more important that you speak up and take charge of the situation.

Tip 52

Be unpredictable

- *"I wonder how the VP will react."*

- *"Will our Director like this report?"*

The above questions are typical in any organization. They reveal a trait typical of all high-powered executives. They like to keep you guessing. They are unpredictable. *Unpredictability* is the hallmark of successful leaders. If you cannot keep others guessing, then you are just "one of them." You cannot afford to be "one of them" if you wish to be seen as someone different.

Being unpredictable does not mean saying something different for the sake of saying something different. It means not taking positions too fast on any issue. Take your time. Use silence as a weapon. Understand all the facts by active listening. Finally, when the timing is just right and people least expect it, speak up! Ask the one question that no one would have. Say something that is profoundly insightful. Be different. Be unpredictable.

Tip 53

Know when to shut up

When to speak up and when to shut up is an important skill to master. To decide when to speak or not, answer two questions:

- *Is the topic at hand of importance to me?*
- *What are the odds of my winning?*

A simple way to decide when to shut up is when one of the following two conditions is met:

- *You don't care!*

- *You do care, but the odds of winning are pretty low.*

Tip 54

No alibis

Success in your career depends greatly on how you react to your failures. One of the most important rules that star employees operate by is the rule of *No alibis*, which means no failure justifications using a bunch of "If" statements. If you start justifying your failure using statements like "if I had just one more month…," or "if I had just one more person in my team…," or "if that other team had delivered in time…," etc., etc. Get the drift?

Tip 55

Be comfy looking dumb

Jack Welch makes a profound statement in his book *Winning*.

> *"When you are a leader, your job is to have all the questions. You have to be incredibly comfortable looking like the dumbest person in the room. Leaders ask questions like 'What if?,' 'Why not?' and 'How come?' Questioning, however, is not enough. You have to make sure your questions unleash debate and raise issues that get action."*

So, do not fear that you will be perceived as being dumb for asking basic questions. The basic questions often help conceive the most original and creative solutions.

Tip 56

Choose the right boss

You will be a lot more successful if you work for someone who has your career goals as part of his or her agenda. With good bosses, the relationship never seems short-term or transactional. Instead, it is active, real, and takes a long-term view of your career goals into consideration. If you do not have this relationship with your current boss, it is a sign to hop and find a different boss.

Tip 57

Be "ha-ha" funny

Carry a sense of humor with you that showcases your belief that there is more to life than just hitting bottom-line metrics. Research has shown that employees laughing three times more often are significantly more productive than their non-laughing counterparts. This may explain why it is rare to find an executive or leader who does not have a sense of humor.

Tip 58

Think like a CEO

The more you think and operate like the CEO of your company, the better your chances of upward mobility and career success. When you make business decisions, ask fundamental questions like:

- *What is the business case behind this decision?*
- *Does the decision increase revenues?*
- *Does the decision decrease costs?*

- *Is this decision simply a market capture or top-line play?*

To think and talk like a CEO, you have to understand the language of business. You should read business magazines, business newspapers and all the classic business books.

Remember, top executives live, breathe and talk a certain jargon. You have to get comfortable with that, and start making that language a part of your daily communication style.

Tip 59

Be a process expert

In recent times, processes have become a key competitive differentiator. The same product being delivered in a different way or form has become a killer mantra for corporate success. Companies like Amazon™, eBay™, Netflix™, Dell™ and a host of others have essentially developed amazingly superior processes to deliver the same product. Understand processes in your organization from a value chain perspective. Evaluate areas in the value chain that are inefficient and ineffective, and design solutions to make them better. Find a lot of process improvement opportunities, and thereby your personal brand.

Tip 60

The back-pocket panacea

Remember that life need not be fair, despite all the strategies that you have developed and executed with finesse. While you travel through your career journey, always remember that the world is not revolving around your goals. Every person's actions are centered with the mission of achieving his or her goals in life.

Below is a back-pocket panacea. Print it and keep it with you at all times as a handy reference.

My back-pocket panacea

- I realize that every action by every person has a self-directed motive. That is a universal fact of life.

- I will not sweat over outcomes that I have no control or influence over.

- The only thing that I truly have total power and control over is my reactions to life's outcomes.
  No one can take away that power from me.

Index

"wow" project, 37
30% Support Rule, 52
30-30-30-10, 19
active listening, 79
Amazon, 91
Anti-Hopping Forces, 32
Benz, 61
Blue-chip, 24
BMW, 61
boiled frog, 29
Canadian geese, 44
Change Agents, 46
compass, 14
C-Zone, 13, 14, 31
Darwin, 23
Dell, 91
differentiate yourself, 41, 75
Dwight Eisenhower, 57
eBay, 91
Google, 27
hop, 30, 32, 34, 87
Hop Zone, 26
ideavirus, 58
Jack Welch, 68, 85
Judy Gilbert, 27
Kia, 61

loss aversion, 59
MBA, 20, 31, 32, 34
mini-goals, 54
Netflix, 91
Niels Bohr, 42
No alibis, 83
opinion coalitions, 70
organization, 13
passion, 13, 14, 15, 50, 74
personal brand, 92
PowerPoint, 56
process improvement, 92
Roger Federer, 72
ROT league, 17
script driven, 70
Seth Godin,, 58
shut up, 7, 81
speak up, 77, 79, 81
Sprezzatura, 71, 72
table stakes, 16
talent, 13, 15
Tom Peters, 50
Toyota, 61
WIIFM, 48
work-life balance, 12, 25

Acknowledgments

Many thanks to my wife, Anita, for her suggestion and constant support to get this pocketbook edition out as a quick reference book of the tips to career success. She never hesitates to make the many cups of coffee that I constantly demand ... all with a smile on her face!.

Thanks also to my superb editor, Jewell Dinneen, who continues to do the job of editing the book to perfection...as always.

About the Author

Ram Iyer is a management professional with diverse experience in various management roles in the automotive, consumer electronics and technology sectors. Over a career span of roughly two decades, Ram has held positions in engineering, operations management, project management, strategic advisory roles, process re-engineering and people management.

Ram was born and raised in the city of Mumbai where he earned his Bachelor's in Engineering from the University of Mumbai passing with Distinction and a University rank holder. After a short stint in corporate India, he moved to the United States to pursue a Master of Science in Industrial Engineering. After a 6 year stint in corporate America, he went to school again to pursue a Master's in Business Administration.

Ram is employed in a management role with one of the leading technology companies in the United States of America.

For any comments or feedback, please contact the author directly at thecareerjourney@gmail.com.

www.ingramcontent.com/pod-product-compliance
Lightning Source LLC
Chambersburg PA
CBHW030916180526
45163CB00004B/1854